THE STUDENT'S MUSIC LIBRARY

Edited by Percy M. Young

MESSIAH

A Study in Interpretation

THE STUDENT'S MUSIC LIBRARY

MESSIAH

A Study in Interpretation

PERCY M. YOUNG, D.MUS.

LONDON
DENNIS DOBSON LTD

First published in Great Britain in MCMLI by
DENNIS DOBSON LTD, London. *All rights reserved*.
Printed in Great Britain by BRISTOL TYPESETTING
COMPANY, Stokes Croft, Bristol 1.

215/R

CONTENTS

CONTENTS

MESSIAH
A Study in Interpretation

PREFACE

THERE ARE TWO words commonly used in
casual observation on Handel or Handelian performance: majesty (or dignity) and simplicity. Both
tend to mislead. Handel was, in fact, neither exclusively
majestic nor exclusively simple. His emotional range
was in every way extensive. His expression, however,
was subtle, and not less so because he was economical
in method.

The qualities of Handel—among which I reckon
tenderness to be most conspicuous—are only evident
when left in Handel's own language. Now this opinion
is not based on abstract principles but on practical
experience. Nor, fortunately, is this experience limited
to work amongst the intelligentsia. I have a force of
butchers, bakers, candlestick makers, their wives and
daughters to testify to the thrilling nature of Handelian
performance according to fundamental principles.

What follows is an account of actual productions
of *Messiah*. This is prefaced by a brief argument so
disposed as to indicate the necessity for some fresh
thought, by *music-makers,* on the interpretative problems.

I hate to think of the number of careless performances of *Messiah* that take place. Performances, that

is, which are encrusted in convention, which invite us to be reverent as before a tomb.

The great characteristic of Handel is his eternal, vibrant liveliness. Let us, then, consider the way in which we may best express this liveliness.

Handel's own suggestions (so far as we have them) seem to me not less but more practicable than those of the ' sapient trouble-tombs ' of later date. I have the feeling that the matters discussed herein would be treated more respectfully were performances with the common additions to the scoring advertised thus: *Messiah,* Handel arr. Mozart (and others).

This is intended as a practical guide-book and not as an academic treatise. In the end it is the Joneses and the Smiths who have to deal with Handel's choral music and I think he would have liked it this way. But he would have hated to be misunderstood.

P. M. Y.

Christmas 1950

I

THE WORK AS A WHOLE

'MESSIAH' LOVERS MAY be divided into four groups. There are some, actuated by a strong religious sense, who regard the oratorio as a statement of faith, as an exposition of Protestant philosophy. Others, immune from this influence and probably increasing in number, are content to regard, more or less exclusively, the musical content of a great work of art. A third group, conspicuous in choral strongholds, are conscious of a particular entertainment value, which may be enhanced by the participation of 'popular' singers. Last comes the minority, able to synthesise all these approaches, to appreciate Handel's attitude, to realise the unique quality of *Messiah* in so far as England is concerned.

Performers and conductors should, but often do not, belong to the last group. Some general advance in self-criticism, in knowledge and in imagination would lead to a more vital appreciation of the corner-stone of general musical experience. There would also follow improvement in choral standards, which we are too often content to accept as higher than they are, and in musical intelligence.

The principles which guide the mode of interpretation to be exposed in this handbook increase, rather than lessen, the pleasure (if the word may, for want of a better, be allowed) of the devout, the artistic, the hedonist and the more generally philosophic.

As this sets out to be a practical work we will immediately turn to the practical; noting, however, that the non-performer may read on, to benefit as much or as little as his more active companion.

It is necessary at the outset to dismiss sentimentality. This atrocious national characteristic leads the faithful to Mr Handel as to the vicar at a sewing meeting: unctuous effusion was as distasteful to the one as it often is to the other. In performance sanctimony generally cloaks incompetence. Let it be dismissed. Freed from what is alleged to be a 'religious style', the performer has taken a step forward.

But having taken a step forward our performer must take a good many backward. A sensitive artist regards each performance—even of a familiar work—as a new, and indeed as a unique performance. This suggests what is particularly important in this context. There is no absolute in interpretation. There is no one way. This was recognised by Handel himself.

There are, however, certain values enshrined in any music. These values must not be obscured.

We must, accordingly, be prepared to examine *Messiah* afresh. Once we regard it as a new work we make discoveries. We find that much of what we have taken for granted is error.

If you are a choral singer, be honest. Do you *know* whether you sing the right notes in *Messiah*? Or do you merely, to quote from an eminent contemporary, ' have a go '? Now right notes are not the end but the beginning. You know the rules of football. Alas! that does not qualify you as a footballer.

Referees and musical scholars, I discover, have a good deal in common. Ill-rewarded for their pains, they are Aunt Sallies for performers and spectators alike. About musical scholarship; this is valuable if it has in mind musical performance; much less valuable if restricted either to what is never likely to be heard or to what never ought to be heard. The aim of the scholar should be to enable both performer and listener to see a score through the composer's eyes. In the case of a work which is two hundred years old, his task is both arduous and important.

The essentials are these: period, people, resources. The eighteenth century had a particular conception of music. The intended audience had special significance and the form of the music took into account the capabilities of individual singers and players. The orchestration was as it was because Handel considered what was immediately, rather than distantly, available.

Most of these points have, historically, been discussed by me elsewhere.[1] We may, however, note one of our major difficulties. Handel's contemporaries were accustomed to a high degree of extemporisation. We do not, therefore, know exactly what additions singers made by way of ornamentation of the written score.

[1] *Handel*. (Master Musicians Series: Dent) *The Oratorios of Handel*. (Dennis Dobson).

We do not know in detail what the harpsichordist played, nor the organist, (although as a rule the organist helped out the chorus singers). We suspect that the leading violin and the cello occasionally added cadenzas. Though, again, we cannot be certain.

Absolute fidelity to Handelian performance is impossible. The case of the academic purist is stillborn. At the same time we can aim at coming as near to the original intentions as our resources will admit. Some latitude is clearly permissible—as in the eighteenth century. But there are frontiers which are not to be crossed.

The great glory of sixteenth-century music is that it is sixteenth-century music. Therefore we do not rescore Palestrina or Byrd. What is generally true of the sixteenth century should be equally true of the eighteenth century. Now many Handelian performances are a betrayal of trust. The eighteenth century has been altered at all points. *Messiah* is made to conform with alien principles. The country road is obliterated. A trunk road, unlovely and unloved, takes its place. Progress loses virtue when arrogant.

Our trunk road ignores detail and blots out scenic subtlety. The too-strong choral society is often completely insensitive to the finer detail of Handel. Its tradition has been that Handel's choruses are bluff, hearty, overwhelming. Now it is true that the music in question may, at times, overwhelm. This, however, is not a matter of numbers, but of style.

The acrobatic mode often adopted by conductors

14

who ought to know better should be mentioned as a factor which sets up false ideals. The popular conductor discovers, quite frequently, that his gesturing, attached to a maximum of noise, pays handsome dividends in careless applause. Therefore *Messiah* must have its trombones, its organ reeds, and the rest of the conventional *addenda*.

Handel's delicacy, his sense of particular orchestral colour, his verbal felicity, his dramatic brilliance (which is not related to noise) are lost. The German, Italian, English influences which are called upon by the composer for their value in emotional association are overrun.

The eminent conductor who sometimes is aware of the problems is content with the line of least resistance. ' Does it matter? People know what they want. Let's give it to them. Don't waste your time on abstract matters. What is more important, don't waste mine!' A ten minute interview with Handel would leave many of the self-satisfied less so. Handel knew his own mind in respect of music.

The evidence we have suggests that libretti for oratorios were considered much more than casually by Handel. We may, profitably, examine the text of *Messiah* before undertaking performance of the oratorio.

In reading the words we become conscious of the unity of the text. This unity depends on variety; on change of emphasis, rhythm, verbal colour; on contrast between epic, lyric and philosophic expression. It

15

may be worth while, privately, to *speak* the text (with four solo speakers and speech chorus) to realise anew its power and its beauty. This experiment will demonstrate, so far as the words alone are concerned, the extent to which the imagination may be fired without recourse to interpretative ostentation.

The music amplifies the thought inherent in the text. It does not merely adorn. Handel, as always, speaks from within his narrative.

Having read the text it will be apparent how deliberately the placing of recitative, aria, arioso, chorus *and* orchestral detail was determined. Consideration of the text will indicate, inevitably, the approach to general interpretation. Look, for instance, at 'O thou that tellest', 'His yoke is easy', 'He trusted in God', 'Let us break their bonds asunder'. On the one hand there is lyric, on the other dramatic intensity. The pattern of the text reinforces Handel's explicit direction (by omission of *da capo*) that the last-named chorus should follow immediately the preceding aria.

Comparison of Handel's libretto with the Authorised Version reveals points of interest. There are certain omissions calculated to make for easier musical fluency. For example:

Every valley shall be exalted, and every mountain and hill [shall be] made low; [and] the crooked [shall be made] straight, and the rough places plain.

(Isaiah xl. v. 4).

16

And though [after my skin] worms destroy this body, yet in my flesh shall I see God.

(Job xix. v. 26).

Sometimes additions are made.

He that *dwelleth* in the heavens shall laugh *them to scorn*: the Lord shall have them in derision.

(Psalm ii. v. 4).

This example—*dwelleth* for *sitteth*—shows eighteenth-century propriety manifest. Other substitutions of an archaic phrase by one more intelligible and, at the same time, more singable may be noted. We may quote:

'He is the righteous Saviour' in place of 'He is just, and having salvation'; 'He trusted in God that He would deliver Him: let Him deliver Him, if He delight in Him' in place of 'He trusted on the Lord that He would deliver Him: let Him deliver Him, seeing He delighted in Him'. 'Behold, I tell you a mystery' in place of 'Behold, I show you a mystery'.

The work of Jennens[2] in preparing the text was admirable. His emendations were scrupulous in that the sense of the original was unaltered. In listening to *Messiah* we do not realise the numerous points of difference. So much trouble having been taken with the words in the first place, we, in performance, should not fail to make them clear. This is not merely a matter of 'diction'; it concerns the symbolic and aesthetic significance of language.

In the chorus 'Lift up your heads' it is often con-

[2] It is probable that Handel made suggestions with regard to the words, particularly in respect of their musical potentiality.

17

ventional to sing 'Who is the King of Glory?' The
Authorised Version has 'Who is this King of Glory?'
Jennens and Handel left this form. Clearly—apart
from authenticity, which can hardly be denied as a
firm ally—there is a demonstrative and dramatic
salience. For this reason 'this' should be restored. The
editions in common use are at fault.

More depends on this demonstrative than technical
accuracy. There is implied the whole Handelian con-
cept of urging the eye, prompted by the ear, to work.
The operatic basis of oratorio should not be forgotten.
The *Compleat Musical Dictionary* attached to my copy
of *Apollo's Cabinet: or the Muses' Delight,* which was
published before Handel died, elucidates oratorio
thus: *a sort of spiritual opera, full of dialogues, recitatives, duettos, trios, ritornellos, choruses, etc.*

If we suggest that *Messiah* (and the companion
oratorios) should be treated, within its own limits,
operatically, this is not to detract from but to add to its
spiritual significance. An opera to convince must be
made alive. An oratorio similarly must be made alive.
The difference between Handel's oratorios and those
of his imitators lies precisely in the liveliness which
belongs to the one and is absent from the other.
Messiah is, at first perhaps, elusive from the operatic
point of view. None the less it is operatic.

Examination of the text—to the feeling of which
Handel is sensitive in every detail—reveals a series of
climaxes. Musically each climax is differently realised.
'Glory to God' calls for additional orchestral colour

but a quiet choral opening. 'He trusted in God' is savage and intensive. 'Hallelujah' brilliant and extensive. 'Amen' is pontifical. Behind the interpretation of these choruses there must be the same sense of vision which inspired their creation. Contemporary performance, after all, is re-creation.

It is improper to take a three act opera and to reproduce it in two acts merely for the sake of convenience. No self-respecting producer would lay himself open to criticism in this respect. Yet *Messiah* is often divided by an interval after 'Lift up your heads'. When this is done the character of the three separate parts goes unrealised.

Then there are cuts. The whole work, provided that time is not wasted, takes approximately three hours. I cannot think that this is longer than intelligent people can endure. If the oratorio is taken seriously—as a complete statement—the general omissions are artistically inadmissible.

To leave out 'He gave His back to the smiters' is to ignore the most poignant moment. 'Thou art gone up on high' is essential to the narrative. As for the choruses which are cut, the apparent reason is often the inability of the singers to sing them.

If performances must be suited to the exigencies of modern transport systems, it is suggested that 'Worthy is the Lamb' should follow, immediately, 'The trumpet shall sound'—complete with *da capo*.

Dr J. M. Coopersmith proposes these emergency excisions:

'Thus saith the Lord of hosts'—'And He shall purify' (inclusive).

'Then shall the eyes of the blind be opened'.

'Thou art gone up on high' (From which I dissent).

'Let us break their bonds asunder'—'He that dwelleth in heaven'.

'The trumpet shall sound' (second part).

'If God be for us'.

I would add that Dr Coopersmith 'feels that a complete performance of *Messiah*, at least once a year, not only is artistically feasible, but also would be musically rewarding. It is not uncommon for concert-goers to hear the complete *Saint Matthew Passion* of Bach at regular intervals; but how many have ever heard a complete performance of *Messiah*? . . . Approached as a *musical* experience, a complete *Messiah* performance would do much to counteract the false traditions that have surrounded this work . . . It should be emphasised that it is far better to perform one part in its entirety than to present a distorted conception of the whole work.'

With all of which I agree.

II

THE CHORUSES

I T IS APPROPRIATE to consider, from the interpretative side, the choruses first. Four competent soloists (engaged at large expense) are hardly likely to give of their best if the choral background is artistically offensive. Nor will an orchestra, whether professional or amateur, consider its contribution carefully unless it is evident that the choir is doing so.

There are more than twenty choruses. The number is sometimes reduced by allowing 'Since by man came death' and 'For as in Adam all die' to the quartet of soloists. I suspect that difficulties of *pianissimo* and intune singing often advise this sentimental departure from Handel's score. Keep the choir if the full solemnity of the phrases is to be understood.[3]

None of the twenty-odd choruses is easy. On the contrary they are all difficult and require lengthy and intensive rehearsal. Never, therefore, rely on those who 'know the music'. They never do.

Note accuracy depends on individual effort. Each singer should learn the coloratura in particular as homework. The necessary foundation is soft tone. This again is contrary to frequent experience. A singing

[3]C.f. a similar and even finer sequence in the *Funeral Anthem*: 'Their bodies are buried in peace'—'But their name liveth for evermore.'

teacher of Handel's day had this to say which is apposite: 'The higher the Notes, the more it is necessary to touch them with Softness, to avoid Screaming'.

Further, the strongest and most subtle rhythmic sense must be brought to bear. The first chorus illustrates every point.

PART I

And the glory of the Lord.

The key of A major is in itself a climax, following the E minor of the overture and the warmer E major of the first recitative and air. The opening should be dynamically restrained—*p* rather than *f*—because (1) there is a climactic sense implicit in the music; (2) the text speaks of the future—'shall be revealed'. Handel adds no dynamic marks, not because he didn't want them, but because, being his own conductor, he could determine these details during rehearsal.

The warmth of this movement depends on the quality of the phrasing: all suggestion of accents on the first beat of every bar should be avoided. This treatment of the key phrases is proposed.

And the glor-y the glor-y of the Lord

In (a) the second 'glory' should be more important than the first. The elision (in somewhat Italian treatment of English) 'glory-of' avoids the hardness of

$$ \text{glo-ry of} $$

and, in fact, approximates more nearly to speech rhythm.

In (b) the word 'all' deserves clarification.

In (c) the tenors and basses should start quite softly, building up by a controlled *crescendo* to the climax of the verb. The rhythm given here (for bar 96) is correct; that in most editions incorrect.

In the contrapuntal passages the voices should float rather than batter their way in. Provided that the phrasing is sensitive, each part will be noticeable.

Make a *crescendo* in bars 36-7 to enhance the modulation. The sopranos from bars 99-102 should feel the cross rhythm. For the soprano entry in bar 106 I

23

always allow myself a slight *ritenuto* over the words 'and the glory'. This is a matter of taste. The high notes at the end of this phrase need nursing. The glory of the Lord is somewhat reduced by earnest ladies who continue to sing although their range effectively stops at G sharp. Those who cannot sing A alone should not be deluded into the belief that they can manage it in company with others.

Tenors and basses should be restrained from bar 130. Because they are moving while the upper parts stand still they will be heard. Finally: either

hath spo - - ken it -

or   Adagio

hath spo - ken it.

Handel did not fix an *adagio* notice on the former version. To continue to the end rhythmically indicates that what the Lord hath spoken He hath also meant. Sharp, incisive, and allowing no question.

Brightness and vitality count far more than loudness; therefore keep below *ff*, even at the very end.

And He shall purify.

Handel borrowed the musical material from a duet for two sopranos and figured bass (*Quel fior che all' alba ride*).[4] This is a purely musical movement. The

[4] Completed on July 1, 1741.

element of purification is best explained by wiping mud from the unfortunate semiquavers. Take *moderato* rather than *allegro* as the norm of speed. The soprano opening is (originally) supported only by figured bass. The strings enter *piano* (Handel) at the end of the second bar. Now Handel would not have had his sopranos arriving *forte* in these conditions. Nor should we. Besides the nature of the text is ferial rather than festal. Whenever the figure

and He shall puri-fy

occurs, make the *crescendo*. The principle that no two notes should be exactly the same is sound practice. Basses are requested for particular discretion. They should endeavour to match the colour and nuance of the sopranos. Similarly tenors and contraltos.

Let the contraltos through in bars 15 and 16, and 19 and 20. Take 'that they may offer unto the Lord an offering in righteousness' in one breath. A break midway wrecks the phrase and makes nonsense of the words. Care should be taken of the sopranos at bar 25 where the delicacy of the entry is charming when realised.

Go on to the end *in tempo*. Nothing is more discourteous to the strings than to imply, by a great choral *rallentando,* that the concluding *ritornello* is really unnecessary. Some old-fashioned conductors, who held orchestras to be at best a necessary evil, cut out such *ritornelli* and filled the missing bars with applause.

A final *rallentando* is a powerful weapon, to be used but seldom—and never negligently.

O Thou that tellest good tidings to Zion.

. Here we arrive at the key of exaltation—D major— which is to dominate the oratorio. There is, however, a pastoral quality in this movement, enhanced by the rhythm, which should not be obscured by enthusiasm. The chorus grows out of the air and there should be no break between. Handel makes his entry *forte*. Of this I would say that expression marks are relative rather than absolute, and I always have rather less than other people's *forte* at the outset. Allow for a *crescendo* in bars 113-4. Make sure that the figure

is clearly defined. Note the words—*Behold, risen.* The contraltos should be allowed precedence in bar 122. Drop the tone a little where all the voices enter at the end of bar 124, but build up mightily to the end. In bar 133 the first chord has the duration

in all parts. Handel left his contraltos with a clear field on the last quaver.

There is in this air and chorus a wonderful sense of radiance. Any performance which gives the sense of light is a valid performance. It will be of necessity sensitive. Chapter xl in the Book of Isaiah is an incomparable poem. Its wealth of imagery is at no time obscured by Handel.

For unto us a Child is born.

At the fourth bar the sopranos enter above the figured bass, which, together with the succeeding figure in the upper strings is marked *piano*. To the end of the first soprano statement the accompaniment is very light. The three bars and a half of semiquavers *must* be within one breath and very gentle. Throughout treat

as marked here. Pick up after the rests as though the vocal line is coming out of the instrumental pattern. Avoid 'a Son is given' . . . explosion . . . 'unto us' . . . another explosion . . . 'a Son is given' . . . In other words, allow the musical texture prominence over diction. Where words are repeated in eighteenth-century music, it is often to allow purely musical development. The rhythm

must be absolutely accurate, but not pedantic to this degree:

♪ ⅞ ♪ ♪ ⅞ ♪ *etc.*

The phrasing must be preserved. The tenor semibreve in bar 28 benefits from

< >

A long note should never be regarded as emotionally negligible.

'Wonderful, counsellor . . .' This occurs four times. I always make the principal effort at the statement in C major. I do not let everything loose at the first ejaculation because, if we follow Handel's score, there is a wonderful halo thrown round the words by the strings which have been, purposefully, kept silent for four bars. In bar 73 *et seq.* the sopranos and contraltos should indulge in sufficient combined rehearsal to ensure that the semiquavers of the one group are of the same length and strength as those of the other.

The basses need, in this movement, continual assurance that they are *gentle*-men. That high E in bar 24 is often quite shocking.

This chorus evolved from the chamber duet *Nò, di voi non vo fidarmi.*[5]

Glory to God.

This is for a choir of angels at some distance. The trumpets are—*da lontano e un poco piano.* I put them off stage. As it is the first movement in which they

[5]July 3, 1741.

28

(should) play there is no practical difficulty. Although the first time I tried this I had to send a bass singer to dig the trumpeters out of their retreat.

'Glory to God' comes three times. The angels come nearer to the earth. The first time we hear them *mp*, the last time—permissibly, I think—*ff*. The phrase 'and peace on earth' should be up rather than down. Peace can be, should be, and was to Handel a positive rather than a negative virtue. This is a sentiment to be issued manfully. Keep bars 27 and 28 within one breath. The sequences in bars 35-38 should be intensified with a *crescendo*. Do not make the crotchets too staccato.

The first contralto note in bar 23 was nearly **A**. Mercifully the master spotted the crime, put what we have now—even though it made a mess on the page—and avoided Consecutive Octaves.

His Yoke is easy.

With this the tender character of Part I is concluded. The music carries into itself the picture of the Good Shepherd. But this is no Holman Hunt representation. Handel's Jesus has grace, athletic ease, humour. In fact he allows to God those virtues often subtracted by the godly.

The key words are 'easy' and 'light'. Feel the literal significance of the second and the first will become an attribute of the singing.

The opening phrase, again delivered against figured bass only, should run somewhat as follows:

His yoke is ea - - - - - sy, His burthen is light,

It is most important that the coloratura throughout is fluid and soft—not 'ea-hea-hea-hea . . . sy', which is the sort of example too frequently set by singers who should know better. The sopranos can make this a movement of the greatest beauty by extreme delicacy in the matter of the high B flats. I think sadly of the sopranos who try this note and shouldn't.

Treat bars 38-40 thus:

His bur - - - - - then is light,

Thus the significance of the crotchets is amplified and the visual sense is satisfied. The final bars should be in strict time as the changed note values make a *rallentando*. Any more would be excessive. Do not make these bars sound merely formal. Try:

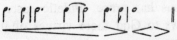

This again is a borrowed movement from the duet *Quel fior che all' alba ride*.[6] Those movements which were once chamber music retain much of the quality of chamber music. This should be borne in mind in performance.

[6]See p. 24.

30

The first part of the oratorio, self-contained, leads from awful anticipation to genial, affectionate delight. If we may use the word, understanding of the music and of the idea within the music is not impossible. There is an intimacy in the communication which brings the subject directly within personal experience. We often speak of Handel's directness, but this it is possible to misappreciate. Handel used what was a commonplace diction, but in his hands it did not seem commonplace. When, however, our performers flatten the diction to suit *their* conception of 'directness' some of the rare quality is lost.

Above Part I floats a delicacy of line, colour and sensibility. One may be reminded of the Botticelli *Nativity* in the National Gallery. In such reminiscence is recollected the generous influence of the Italian renaissance, to which Handel—as Botticelli—was indebted.

In the second part a different set of values prevails. The colours are darker, the rhythms sterner. Handel as a connoisseur of painting collected pictures by Rembrandt. In the tragic passages of *Messiah* may aptly be recalled what Henri Dumont drew attention to in Rembrandt—'his profound humanity and mysterious emotional appeal'.

PART II

Behold the Lamb of God.

Immediately the 'profound humanity' is evident.

31

Handel points as the Man of Sorrows passes. He uses a musical symbolism which was in his own day even more definitive than today. The jagged rhythm

♪ ♪ ♪ ♪ ♪ ♪

put in minor tonality turns the mind towards tragedy.[7] The choir must preserve this inexorable rhythm at all costs. Inexorability equally depends on highly competent breath control. There are long held notes for the sopranos which must not be allowed to weaken. The phrase 'that taketh away the sin of the world' must always come within one breath—which requires considerable practice. Although the edges of the rhythm must be clear the phrases must also be sung *legato*, otherwise much of 'the mysterious emotional appeal' is missed.

Each part should show its own perception of the colour of the phrases. The crucial word is 'sin', which calls not so much for a conventional accent as a higher degree of emotional pressure. The climactic 'Behold the Lamb of God', as the music shows, is in bars 16 and 17. A more impassioned atmosphere should prevail at this point. Then the transition to E flat major follows (rather softer) with sublime sympathy.

The last two tenor notes in bar 6 read

♪ ♪

[7] C.f. 'My Father, if indeed it may be' (*Passion* (No. 2.) Handel).

in the autograph. Bar 18 reads, in the soprano,

Basses often misinterpret the E natural in the eleventh bar and admit E flat.

Surely, He hath borne our griefs.
And with His stripes we are healed.

Together with the first chorus of this section and the succeeding air these make a wonderful triptych.

Surely, He hath borne our griefs, heightens the tragedy. The rhythm is more fierce and must again be entirely accurate. The transition to the relative major widens the sympathy because the figure

is thrown behind the commiseration of the voices. The first word of great significance—both musically and for its own sake—is *griefs.* At the end of the eighth bar the word can carry, effectively, a *crescendo.* The succeeding passage must be full, rich and unhurried, a *crescendo* leading at bar 15 to the next distinctive word—'bruised'. Obviously the tempo must not slacken as the voices end.

In the fourteenth bar basses are advised to take the upper C very lightly.

The fugal chorus should begin immediately. The

subject has a sombre quality:[8] the eighteenth century was accustomed to this subject as possessing a particular emotional suggestiveness. The fugal repetition of this subject makes further delineation unnecessary. While sorrow is maintained the interest primarily is musical. In the preceding movements realism has been exhausted. To allow time for emotional and philosophic reflection by the interpolation of a fugue was common Handelian practice.[9]

A guide to the required breadth of phrasing comes from Handel, who wrote the movement in bars which contained not two but eight minims.

The temptation should be resisted to end this movement *ff*. There are greater climaxes to come and there is no need to emulate those organists who must couple the Solo Tuba for the end of everything. A diapason tone *forte* can be extraordinarily telling. The *Adagio* bars may be taken exactly in time but with the note values doubled in length. Do not, on any account, add *adagio* and *rallentando*.

Contraltos often take advantage of a careless conductor and prefer A natural to A flat at the end of bar 97.

All we like sheep.

Here Handel has fallen back on his chamber music. The same duet which provided material for *For unto us a Child is born* serves again. The implication, therefore, is lightness.

[8]C.f. 'Kyrie' (*Requiem*—Mozart).
[9]C.f. middle section of the great 'Jealousy' chorus in *Hercules*.

Blasted out, *con tutta forza*, the first part of this exquisite movement sounds incongruous. *All we like—elephants*? No! this is a *scherzo*. Musically some relaxation is required at this point. As for the text, Handel stands outside human affairs momentarily and sees the sinful with amused affection. He regards the sheep-like as an adult a pack of naughty little boys. He also sees the sheep.

I must confess to interpreting the opening phrase thus:

For the rest the counterpoint unwinds with natural nuance—without that perspiring agitation which so often brings from the tenor contingent an unintended note of angry expostulation.

The rout ceases. Comedy changes to tragedy again. Or rather the tragedy within the comedy steps out. The quavers and semiquavers are ended. Longer notes in a slow tempo take their place.

And the Lord hath laid on Him the iniquity of us all.

In this abrupt change Handel's consummate genius is seen. Now to go to sentimental extremes is unnecessary. The voices should *not* be left unaccompanied. Handel reserves that for a further solemn gesture. Nor, I think, should the music die beyond a firm *piano*. What matters here is breath control. Most of the breathing places are marked by punctuation. Seven bars from the end, however, the dominant seventh and its resolution must be within one breath. Clearly this is desirable both musically and verbally. The last nine soprano bars are quoted.

hath laid on Him, on Him the i-ni-qui-ty of us all.

It is possible to dispense with the last breathing place with advantage to the phrasing. The problem with basses and tenors is easier. So far as basses are concerned, breath taken after the long B flat will not be noticed provided that the upper parts are sustained.

It is remarkable how much simpler breathing becomes when time is *not* broken and when proportion *is* kept.

He trusted in God.

We have it on the authority of George III that this was one of the choruses which Handel himself held in the highest esteem. The words, noted the king, 'contain a manifest presumption and impertinence, which Handel has, in the most masterly manner, taken advantage of'. Presumption, impertinence, arrogance, contumely: these are the qualities which must remain in mind when the chorus is sung. I notice my own score marked 'savage'. That was the direction by a great choral conductor from whom I learned. Choral singers must lose their inhibitions. Here is no 'religious' music. Walton comments no more effectively on this side of human nature in *Belshazzar's Feast*. He makes more noise.

Speak the words of the fugue subject to rhythm, taking care 'to shoot out the lip' and to 'shake the head'. In this way the iron grip of Handel on the English language is understood. Yet due expression of verbal emphasis asks no distortion of musical values. Notice the natural *crescendo* which comes with the second 'He'; the hammer blows—Beethoven learned from this side of Handel—

let Him de - li - ver Him

the scornful tremor on the second syllable of 'delight'. These go into the musical interpretation.

Initially it is the sense of overhanging threat which strikes the listener and this is more effective if kept to *mf*. Throughout, singers should resist the temptation to hurry any or all of the notes. I must confess to encouraging derision from the tenors on their long run on 'delight' from bar 43-45. *Staccato* rather than *legato* is exceedingly cutting at this point. The sopranos may let fly with a genuine broadside of contempt at bar 50.

Run straight on without a vestige of *rallentando* until pulled up by the masterly and characteristic rest which prefaces the *Adagio*. Thence, still mocking, to the end in strict, but slower time.

In the next to the last bar the basses should sing

Lift up your heads.

The previous chorus is exhausting. It should be exhausting. By the time its successor arrives, however, this state should have passed. *Lift up your heads* can sound dull. It is in fact one of the weaker movements and needs conscious effort. Every other chorus survives maltreatment: this one is less virile.

It is based on earlier Italian models, being antiphonal.[10] Preserve the contrast between question and answer—which requires the tenors and basses at the outset to keep down. The affirmative passages start very broadly and great dignity should be maintained. Sing the runs, therefore, as smoothly as possible. A particular passage requiring great skill in phrasing is

and the King of glo-ry shall come in,

At * there is frequently an ugly break.

Between bars 26 and 29 the high voices ask their question three times. Make each time of asking more insistent. It may be mentioned here that the effect of Handel's orchestration with *concertino* and *con ripieno* contrasts is both charming and definitive. None but the deaf or the merely stupid would prefer any other

[10]The music is also used in a *Concerto a due Cori* II (c.1748-50).

orchestration, once having heard this characteristic eighteenth-century effect.

Once again continue to the end in strict time, the last three chords arriving as in the timetable. A full blaze illuminates the final scene. The key word throughout has been 'glory'. The vowel sound as used in Yorkshire gives full content.

'Who is *this* King of Glory?'
The second beat for all sopranos in bars 27, 28 and 29 should be

The bass part in bars 69 and 70 is correctly:——

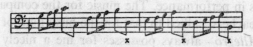

The notes marked * are usually miswritten. In bar 36, the tenors should have

as the last note.

Let all the angels of God.

I am reminded of Mendelssohn's account of Titian's *Assumption*—'the angels . . . encircling Mary with joyous shouts of welcome; one beating the tambourine, a couple of others blowing away on strange crooked flutes, another lovely group singing—or the music floating in the thoughts of the cithern player'.

If ever I go to heaven—which is unlikely—I shall hope to hear an angelic choir perform this chorus with the authentic ethereal brilliance. This is music which is radiant. Consider the passage (with diminution, for this is even academically outstanding) for the high voices from bar 22. A heavy responsibility rests on the sopranos. In the fifth bar sopranos and contraltos must not sound surprised.

The Lord gave the word.

The title phrase should be delivered authoritatively and grandly. Above *forte* as though stated by orchestral brass. The entries sometimes catch the singers unawares in performance. The music for the company of the preachers—allied to that for the busy hum of cities in *L'Allegro*—always possesses for me a nicely vehicular character. A bus load of outlying parsons on their way to a diocesan meeting. Not much can be done to this chorus. The pedestrian effect of

should, however, be avoided.

Their sound is gone out into all lands.

This chorus represents an afterthought. It was an addition to the autograph score. It is a magnificent second thought. Broad, *legato,* full throated singing is required. This chorus shows what counterpoint means. The last eight bars bring its majesty to a carillon conclusion, with scales rising and falling one against the other. The shape of the individual contours is to be shown.

Attention to bars 23 and 24 brings a flood of tone in full spate. Make the rhythm extremely deliberate and extract the richest chordal quality.

Let us break their bonds asunder.

I am afraid the choir *must* stand during *Why do the nations*. Otherwise the tremendous impetuosity of this outburst is lost. There is nothing for the choir to do but to sing the right notes with spirit and determination. Handel's thunderbolts have become legendary. There is a tag to fit this movement.[11]

> *Eripuit coelo fulmen, mox sceptra tyrannis.*
> (He snatched the thunderbolts from heaven,
>   soon the sceptres from tyrants).

By the end of the chorus the power of tyranny should appear diminished. Two wonderfully placed cadential chords call for emphasis in performance—at bars 9 and 34. The studious will notice the stringent effect of the *stretti*.

Hallelujah.

Comparing this with *Let all the angels of God* I must agree with Fitzgerald. This, he wrote, is 'a chorus, not of angels, but of well-fed earthly choristers, ranged

---

[11] which must include the air.

41

tier above tier in a Gothic cathedral . . .' Of course one cannot escape the contagious exuberance of this chorus, but it is not the climactic chorus.

Too often, exuberance outruns musicianship and the resulting exaltation is too nearly akin to that experienced the other day when our footballers equalised in the last half minute. This music is still music. Therefore let the Hallelujahs ring rather than roar. Begin *f* and *ff* throughout with consideration for the rhythmic ricochet. I suggest (with many precedents in Handelian style)

for the Lord God Om-ni - po-tent reign - eth

'The kingdom of this world' should not be reduced to *molto allargando*. I further suggest

is be - come the Kingdom of our Lord and of His Christ, and of His Christ;

A sudden effusion of tone at 'the' sounds unlikely, while something held in reserve for the phrase end gives the basses the right introduction for their subject, which should be announced in rounded tone of great pontifical dignity.

The long held notes of the final section sound better

A big climax occurs at bar 87. The last page must not

be hard but resilient even in loudness. Again treat the end rhythm with exactness.

Audiences who stand for this chorus should not make a noise when so doing. Personally I dislike the practice as it intrudes on the continuity of the music. It is, I fear, habit not respect. I should prefer greater respect for Handel and less for George II's gesture. Or if we must have one eighteenth-century tradition, let us have all the rest. But then logic is not our strong suit.

PART III

The third part of *Messiah,* complete in itself as the first and second parts, is a summary of Christian faith and hope. The exquisite qualities of *I know that my Redeemer liveth* are enhanced when the interval between the acts is allowed.

Since by man came death.

The four short choruses of this section form the theological denouement of the plot. The importance of the moment is indicated by the appearance of chorus unaccompanied. There is no warrant for the use of solo quartet for the minor key utterances. The chorus sounds gravely impersonal. Both *Since by man came death* and *For as in Adam all die* can be delivered in a firm, controlled *pp*, with pressure on the consonant in 'death' and 'die'. Great care must be taken if pitch is to be maintained.

The last two bars of *By man came also the resurrection of the dead* can carry an exhilarating *crescendo*.

In bars 6-9 the bass part should read:

This the basses should prefer.

But thanks be to God.

To be sung with calm dignity. The final *adagio* should be reduced to *f* otherwise the conclusion of the oratorio becomes anticlimactic. The repetition of 'thanks' calls for careful handling if an ugly jingle is to be avoided.

The alto in bar 7 should be

our Lord   Je — sus Christ

Worthy is the Lamb: Amen.

Dignity is the first consideration. But this does not preclude colour.

These points seem to me to be necessary aids to presentation:

1. *Crescendo* on final minim in bar 2, maintaining the integrity of the phrase.

2. Change to *andante* at bar 7; *not* to *allegro*.

3.   to re-ceive pow-er   *not*   to re-ceive pow-wer

4.   From ' Blessing and honour . . . .' concentrate on brilliance and extreme clarity.

5.   Deliver the subject

6.

Blessing, honour, glory, and power,

From the *adagio* run without any break at all into the *Amen* chorus. This deliberate polyphony should be delivered as though for the aisles and ambulatories of some great church. If one suggested that this was Palestrina remodelled for the eighteenth century one might be misunderstood. But if Palestrina is in mind, the greatness of this music is more likely to be realised.

Handel generally marks the group

A - men

thus :

A - men

the *martellato* of which is to contrast with the long *legato* phrases.

The bass part in bars 7—9 reads:

A - - - - - men,

in bars 4—6

A - - men, A - - men,

The alto in bars 58—61

A - men, A - - - - men,

The bass in bars 67—8

A - men, A -men,

This leaves barely room to insist on clean chording, variation of dynamic intensity according to the melodic rise and fall, and no suspicion of coarseness.

These general observations are valid whatever the instrumental accompaniment and however large the choir. It is, however, sufficiently apparent that large numbers are likely to prove a handicap if the characteristic qualities of the music are adequately to be represented. The size of the choir, however, should be related to the conditions of performance. Forty singers are adequate for most buildings—except the Albert Hall. Many promoters of *Messiah* in churches and chapels have a habit of cramming in as many choristers (the choir is nearly always—and this is sinister—'augmented') as possible. Frequently they must sit in grievous discomfort. This ensures bad performance.

A plea, which will not be popular, must be made for young voices, particularly among sopranos. Nine *Messiah* performances out of ten demand an excess of charity on the part of the disinterested, to whom the defects of the superannuated are only too audible. Effective interest often comes from those who have never sung the work before and who are willing to 'start at the beginning'.

There may be expected from a competent choir an ability (a) to sing the notes with detailed accuracy; (b) to colour the phrases as one would colour Verdi or Britten; (c) to sing the choruses in rehearsal without accompaniment.

Finally as to standing up. The continuity of each part must be maintained. The choir can assist by avoiding unnecessary movement. After *And He shall purify* remain standing until the end of *O Thou that tellest*. Stand before *There were shepherds* so that *Glory to God* follows immediately 'praising God, and saying'. Remain standing throughout *All they that see Him* so that *He trusted in God* is properly effective. Stand from the beginning of *Lift up your heads* until the end of *Let all the angels of God*. Stand before *Why do the nations* to be ready for *Let us break their bonds asunder*.

Further, stand *before* the orchestral introductions and not during them. If it is complained that much standing is involved, consider the conductor and the music.

III

SOLOS AND SOLOISTS

A DEFECT IN modern oratorio performance is the customary episodic treatment. To this most principals contribute by preening themselves as the exclusive purveyors of airs and, more unfortunately, recitatives. To hear *Comfort ye; He was despised; Why do the nations; I know that my Redeemer liveth;* is, as a rule, to be impressed with the supposed merits of particular singers rather than the especial power of these movements within their contexts. I am tempted to hand out two governmental nouns: integration and co-ordination. In other words, let no soloist sing a part in *Messiah* without studying the other solos and the choruses. Then each recitative and air can take its proper place.

For three hundred years and more, musicians have advised singers. Thomas Morley was quoted in Handel's day. We may quote him again. 'They [singers] ought to study how to vowel and sing clean, expressing their Words with Devotion and Passion, whereby to draw the Hearer as it were in Chaines of Gold by the Eares to the Consideration of holy Things.' Further to this Morley added what may or may not still be apt: '. . . . having obtained the Living which they sought for, they have little or no Care at all, either of

4

their own Credit, or well discharging of that Dutie whereby they have their Maintenance.'

The best singers of Handel's day did know how to vowel and sing clean. They had other virtues—of brilliance, of *cantabile*, of 'perfect Intonation', and 'Strictness of Time'.[12] Now the last did not imply mechanical strictness. *Rubato* was known, but recognised as an attribute of the greatest musicianship.

'Our author,' comments Mr Gilliard, 'has often mentioned Time; the Regard to it, the Strictness of it, and how much it is neglected and unobserv'd. In this place speaking of stealing the Time, it regards particularly the Vocal, or the Performance on a single instrument in the *Pathetick* and *Tender*; when the Bass goes an exactly regular Pace, the other Part retards or anticipates it in a singular Manner, for the Sake of Expression, but after that returns to its Exactness, to be guided by the Bass. Experience and Taste must teach it. A mechanical Method of going on with the Bass will easily distinguish the Merit of the other Manner.'

Our author Signor Tosi gave this classical definition of *rubato*: ' The stealing of Time, in the Pathetick, is an honourable Theft in one that sings better than others, provided he makes a Restitution with Ingenuity.'

For the moment these observations serve to define the limits of the singer's territory.

[12]Tosi on Faustina and Cuzzoni.

We may proceed to an examination of the airs and recitatives in *Messiah.*

Soprano.

An eighteenth-century soprano was expected to possess brilliance. Brilliance was not to be sacrificed to speed. Cuzzoni, for example, ' had no great rapidity of execution ' but she made up for this by ' her tender and touching expression' and her neatness. Her rival Faustina was conspicuous for an ' execution . . . . articulate and brilliant. She had a fluent tongue for pronouncing words rapidly and distinctly, and a flexible throat for divisions . . . .'[13] Such singers were of the opera, although Cuzzoni ' came back ' for Handel in 1750 to sing in *Messiah.* The standards of vocal excellence set by such singers remained, however, to inspire their successors in oratorio.

It is clear that ability to sing Handelian parts with instrumental efficiency has, on the whole, declined since romantic interpretation has caused admiration for departure from rather than adherence to the details of what Handel wrote.

The sequence of recitative, beginning *There were shepherds,* enchantingly changes the atmosphere of Part I. A soft brilliance is called for. In the accompanied recitatives, the voice set within a garland of string tone, sing the rhythm as written, with no last bar alterations. It will be noticed that the *character* of the soprano voice makes sufficient emotional appeal with-

[13]See Burney: *Travels* II, pp. 188-9.

out the necessity for the singer to do more than sing. The same is true of *Rejoice greatly*. It is customary to drawl the middle section. I cannot think that this is either beautiful or intended. Sufficient contrast with the first part of the air is introduced by minor tonality. Such liberties, added together, make the oratorio tedious.

Passing by *He shall feed His flock* (to be considered under the contralto head), we meet next *How beautiful are the feet*. This—' a very pleasing air, *alla Siciliana*,' should be sung ' with elegant simplicity '. It is important that in these airs based on dance rhythms the movement of the distant dance should not be obscured.

I know that my Redeemer liveth is one of those movements where sentiment is wrongly preferred to accuracy. The great beauty of the air depends on the phrasing. Avoid

♩ |♩ ♩   ♫|
I   know   that

Avoid equally

♩|♩ ♩ ♩|♩ ♩ ♩|♩ ♩ ♩|♩ ♩ |♩♩ ♩|♩♩
for now is Christ ri-sen, for now is Christ ri-sen   from the dead,
                                    (breath)

This, of course, makes nonsense both of music and words. Alteration in Handel's syllabic division is sometimes taken to be expedient. It should be recognised, however, that in an air the *idea* of the text is contained within the character of the music, and that ' speech rhythm ', as a firm control, belongs rather more to the province of recitative.

If God be for us is a fine, strict episode which should be omitted only with regret.

Contralto.

Women contraltos were a new phenomenon in the time of Handel. Male contraltos were excluded from English music because they were frequently a nuisance, but the female voice admitted more emotion. The esteemed quality was the ' pathetic ', to which reference in contemporary writings is often made. It was because she could act with her voice that Mrs Cibber moved the first *Messiah* audiences so considerably.

The basis of the interpretation of the contralto part of *Messiah* is sympathy. *O Thou that tellest* (and the preceding recitative) must be calm, consolatory, hopeful; but above all calm. The phrases must be warm, powerful without force, and the runs must be smooth with accentuation left to the bass. The words of Rabindranath Tagore may be recalled:

O Thou Beautiful! how in the nest thy love embraceth the soul with sweet sounds and colour and fragrant odours!

Were it not invidious I would also be tempted to recall the art of Miss Ferrier, whose objectivity in this air is a model.

He shall feed His flock suffers very much from those I have rudely disguised elsewhere as Miss Soap and Mme Slop. The late Sir Edward Bairstow refers some-

53

where to the use of pastoral music throughout *Messiah*
to keep before the listener the picture of the Good
Shepherd. This movement is often too slow. I must say
that the alteration of

$$\flat \mid \downarrow \smile \; \flat \; \downarrow$$

He shall   feed

to

$$\flat \mid \downarrow \; \flat \; \downarrow$$

He ____ shall feed

denies (a) the rhythm, and (b) the force of the verb.
At bars 9 and 15 Handel wrote

with   His   arm,

He was despised is pointless without the middle section and *da capo*. To perform the air in its entirety
precludes that characteristic dallying by the rests
which takes all the rhythm away. The section *He
gave His back to the smiters* is as tragic as Handel can
be. The final ' from shame and spitting ', to be sung
almost *parlando,* is desperate in agony. This, I suspect, is why it is omitted. The final duet—*O death,
where is thy sting*—in which the contralto is involved
is pedestrian music.

Tenor.

Comfort ye will sound more effective in than out of
time. A tenor I once heard rolled his eyes most agilely
on the first word. This did not add to the musical effect.

The last eight bars are clearly to be treated more dramatically, thus forming a contrasting middle section to a three part movement, of which *Every valley* is the last part. This is not to be hurried. I feel that the voice part can only be displayed properly against Handel's light weight instrumentation.

The tenor part in the passion music is sublime. Although Handel sometimes gave this to a soprano one would prefer to keep the traditional narrative function of the tenor. Throughout Handel intensifies feeling harmonically. If the singer considers intonation then the emotional quality will stand out. I notice that when Mr Norris sang this music at the *Handel Commemoration* of 1784, he was said to have ' preserved the character ' of the music. Which may recommend tenors to avoid trying to put their own personalities within that of Mr Handel. There isn't room.

Thou shalt break them is a magnificent tone poem, calling for great musicianship and the ability to equate the vocal with the instrumental line. A favourite of Handel was John Beard. 'He did not out-Herod Herod . . . he never outstepped the modesty of nature . . . he never did more than was set down for him.' I have learned much about the way to sing Handel from the example of Mr Eric Greene.

Bass.

The chief requisite for the bass singer is a capacity for singing coloratura precisely and easily. The *prestissimo* interpolations in *But who may abide* and the

55

allegro of *Why do the nations* frequently defeat the energetic singer who has not learned to sing. The opportunities for imaginative penetration given to the bass are generous. All the recitatives are finely dramatic; *But who may abide* requires a fine *legato* in the *larghetto, The people that walked in darkness* a sense of great mystery. The cadences in D major in this air are miracles of musical and dramatic climax. *Thou art gone up on high* is, like *Thou shalt break them,* more or less instrumental. It therefore acts as a relief from the more intrinsically and obviously dramatic. It also lessens the brilliance attained by the previous chorus. *Why do the nations* runs its angry course but must lead inevitably, ruthlessly, to the choral conclusion. The expensive bass who insists on a *da capo* is no musician. Nor is he who will have *The trumpet shall sound* in C major. Generally basses tend to miss the pontifical character of this air and aim at overtopping the trumpet solo.

From what has been said it is clear that appreciation of nuance plays a large part in Handelian interpretation. More often than not, however, the singer must approach the music from an instrumentalist's position. He or she must respect, above all, the integrity of the melodic phrase, and must feel it in relation to its intimate setting. This matter of intimacy will be reviewed again under the head of orchestration. It is proper to be dramatic—but not in the nineteenth-century way; in that age too often melodrama displaced drama.

It appears that as Handel matured, his attitude to singers changed. First he looked for virtuosity. In his later oratorio days, however, he chose singers because their voices suited particular parts. But there was this in common between the virtuoso and the interpretative genius of those days. Both were regarded as within their rights in adding to the written score embellishments of their own choosing. Thus[14]

He was de-spis-ed, de-spis-ed and re-ject-ed,

is what Handel is thought to have heard. A further quotation from the same source will prove more surprising:

crook-ed straight and the rough _____ pla-ces plain.

Handel marked a pause. It was to indicate a cadenza passage.

Anton Reicha in *On the Art of Ornamenting* had this to say: ' From the time of Allegri, Leo, and Durante, to that of Hasse and Handel, the manner of singing was at once simple, touching and grand. The singer seldom ventured to employ any other ornaments than the appoggiatura, the trill and some few other passing embellishments, till he came to the *point*

[14]Quoted by Dr. J. M. Coopersmith from the Rosenbach *Messiah* transcript in New York. The ornamentation is said to be in the hands of J. C. Smith, Handel's secretary.

d'orgue at the close of the air, when he considered himself in his own domain.'

We should now tend to regard such digression as trivial. But not in a violin or pianoforte concerto. The singer has been moved from the focal point: that is why he has had his cadenzas removed. I am not sure that it would be a bad thing if the singer were to regain his former prestige. If he did perhaps his ancient rights would be restored.

For the time being, however, we must admit the impracticability of having Handel's airs after his own manner in this respect. The chief difficulty is that we do not, nor ever shall, know exactly what was done. Not that any one song was sung with the same ornamentation by any two singers!

' The first and most principal Grace, necessary to be learned, is the Trill or Shake; that is, to move or shake your Voice distinctly on one Syllable the Distance of either a whole Tone or a Semitone, always beginning with the Note or half Note above . . . .

' The Trill ought to be used on all descending pricked [*i.e.,* printed] Notes, and always before a Close; also on all descending sharpened Notes . . . .

' There is another Grace used in Music, called the Grace of Transition; that is, to slur or break a Note, to sweeten the Roughness of a Leap, etc.'

So even the modest church singer was instructed in the *Complete Psalmodist* of 1769.

Earlier writers were more involved and gave Shakes Major, Shakes Minor, Short Shakes (to add brilliance to ' brisk and lively airs '), Rising Shakes, Descending Shakes (forms of *portamento*), Slow Shakes, Redoubled Shakes, and the Shake with a Beat.

The shake generally added lightness. The appoggiatura had more often a tender or pathetic effect. After the appoggiatura came *Gliding* and *Dragging*—forms of modified *portamento* in which the individual notes could be distinguished—also apt to the Pathetic. After that Divisions, as in the second example on p. 57.

Anyone who can pick up a copy of the songs which were popular at Vauxhall and Ranelagh will find many of the more common ornaments written in.

Formerly appoggiaturas remained in Handel (the edition of *Messiah* by W. T. Best has a number written in). Latterly they have been banished by those who labour under the impression that they are alien to the style. They should, I feel, return.

This matter of ornaments raises the question: if it is impossible to be ' authentic ' in this, why trouble in other matters where precise knowledge, admittedly, helps? One may vary the furniture of a medieval church, indeed—with advantage—one may strip it entirely of recent fittings, but no fundamental alteration of character takes place. Tamper with the structure, on the other hand, and the character is mutilated. Music, like architecture, depends on fine calculations in balance. Upset the balance—as between singers and instrumentalists—and the *structural* proportions are destroyed. Ornaments are non-functional by nature (study of Handel's airs will show that unconsciously he tended to write them in ' pricked ' notes where they assumed greater significance) and can be lost.[15] I repeat, however, that their complete disappearance is a pity if only because with them has departed some of the grace of eighteenth-century vocal music.

[15]We could do without instrumental cadenzas without the meaning of the concerto being seriously affected; sometimes, no doubt, the sterner among us would. But we must not be too moral. Sugar on pills is no bad thing so long as the pill goes down with the sugar.

IV

ORCHESTRATION

O N MARCH 1 1, 1 8 2 9, *Messiah* was performed at Drury Lane. A critic observed:

But to produce this Oratorio now, without the additional accompaniments of Mozart, is either a proof of the most unaccountable make up in the manager, or of an obtuseness in his perception, that cannot be too strongly censured. Mozart . . . only had recourse to means which there is every reason to believe Handel would gladly have employed, had they been within his reach. Mozart . . . has only supposed himself in the great composer's place, and done exactly what he was justly entitled to conclude Handel himself would have done, had he written his *Messiah,* at the close, instead of the early part of the eighteenth century.

The same argument came out yesterday, and the day before. It will come out tomorrow and the day after that. Had Handel lived at any other time he would not have written an oratorio at all.

Dear, poor Handel! The condescension in the ' he would have employed had he had them ' argument is insufferable. In any case it is a bad argument.

Look what Handel did use: four trumpets in *Rinaldo*; three trombones, three bassoons and carillon in *Saul*; a harp in *Esther*; two organs in *Solomon*; lute and mandoline in *Athalia*; nor were clarinets unknown, and percussion commanded his affectionate attention. Handel was, in fact, one of the *avant garde* among orchestrators.

The basis of the Handel orchestra was the string ensemble. So, it may be said, it is today. But there is this difference. The eighteenth-century ear was more conscious of the colour range of the individual instrument. There was not one violin tone. There were, perhaps, fifty. The violin, urged de Beriot in his *Violin School,* is ' capable of simulating all the subtle inflexions of song '. The human voice, he added, was the model for all *played* music. De Beriot was here not being original. He was repeating the classical tenets of Corelli and Geminiani, the twin influences on English string playing during the Handelian epoch.

Geminiani, conspicuous for his ' tender and pathetic ' performance, was a friend of Handel and taught many who played in Handel's orchestras. His *Art of Playing on the Violin* (1730) was an important contribution to eighteenth-century technical improvement. Matthew Dubourg, who led the orchestra in the first performance of *Messiah* and who was regarded as an exceedingly ' bold and rapid ' performer, was a pupil of Geminiani, as was also Michael Festing. Other Handelian violinists came straight from Corelli. There were, in particular, Pietro Castrucci, leader of the opera band until 1737; and Stefano Carbonelli, who led for the oratorios. The musical personality of the leader was as important as that of the singers, as may be seen on examination of the *Messiah* score.

One may therefore see that the frequent use of a solo violin in aria added to rather than detracted from emotional appeal.

In his oratorios (and operas) Handel treated his strings in the familiar manner of the concerto grosso. They were divided into concertino (a solo quartet) and ripieno (the non-solo part of the ensemble).[16] In any circumstances—whether in Corelli and Handel or Elgar, Vaughan Williams or de Falla—the contrast thus given is enchanting.

Oboes and bassoons are confined in *Messiah* to the choruses. The parts which were used in the Foundling Hospital performances at the end of Handel's life were discovered half a century ago and are incorporated in the Prout edition. We may repeat that if Handel had wished for wind co-operation elsewhere he would not have hesitated. Precedents abound.

Handel intended orchestral restraint. This is the significant difference between *Messiah* and the other oratorios. This quality of restraint is precisely what Mozart missed.

Now adherence to Handel gives the sublime and mystical entry of trumpets in *Glory to God*. This is the first trumpet entry. It is some time before there is another. Trumpets, with drums, appear, triumphantly in *Hallelujah* and, finally, in *Worthy is the Lamb* and *Amen*. There is, of course, the solo trumpet in *The trumpet shall sound*. These brass interpolations are

[16]Indications as to where passages should be *senza rip.* and *con rip.* were written by Handel into the score now at St. Michael's College, Tenbury.

thrilling because they are rare. Increase them and the thrill is diminished. Moreover they are high trumpet parts, after the manner of the eighteenth century, and on that account doubly telling.

Behind the choruses lay the firm, resonant and binding tone of the organ. The modern organist is advised to refrain from imagining an organ recital and to confine his registration to diapason and flute tone (16', 8', 4' and 2'). Behind the airs the harpsichord, from which the conductor (Handel) directed the performance.

Here, if we are in search of authenticity, we are defeated. We do not know exactly what was played on the harpsichord. We may, however, suppose that realisation of figured bass was freer and more independent than the humbly utilitarian version of Chrysander. I imagine that Handel allowed his fancy a good deal of latitude in arpeggios, in spontaneous counter melodies, in rhythmic emphasis, and (within limits) in registration. I feel that intuition is of more assistance here than theories derived from text-book analysis. By working at the figured basses of concertos and sonatas one realises that a harpsichord player of the eighteenth century engaged in his occupation with the same self-satisfaction as a medieval sculptor intent on that side of a roof boss which would never be seen. For fine detail or ingenious counterpoint cannot expect to be noticed when the harpsichord is in the background. Merely pedestrian continuo, on the other hand, is obtrusive.

If a harpsichord is not available, either use the organ

(which Handel would have done) or the pianoforte. The obvious disadvantage of the latter is that it is not a harpsichord. On the other hand it is a keyboard instrument of rhythmic vitality—as opposed to the organ—and an *intimate* collaborator.

The separate items in *Messiah* may now be examined in orchestral detail.

Overture: Strings only. The rhythm of the *Grave* introduction may reasonably be accepted as

Double-dotting was generally conventional and such a movement as this was intended as a spur to attention. This *grave* is, however, clearly more than utilitarian music. Both parts of the overture should bear intensity of expression and should on no account be deficient in dynamic range.

Comfort ye: senza rip: bars 1—4, beats 3 and 4 of bar 7 (inclusive).

Every valley: senza rip: bars 1—9, 15—18, 20—23, 26—42 (*con rip,* on last quaver), 46—50, 56—71 (*con rip*. on last quaver).

And the glory: senza rip. until bar 14.

Thus saith the Lord and *But who may abide: senza rip*. throughout. The reiterated semiquavers from the 14th bar with a diminished number of strings and with the rhythmic impulse of the harpsichord (or piano) are very striking in performance.

And He shall purify: senza rip. until bar 15.

O Thou that tellest: the *ripieno* instruments are silent until the last quaver of the second full bar of the chorus.

For behold and *The people that walked in darkness: senza rip.* throughout. Mozart got into trouble for harmonising the opening of the latter. Coopersmith thinks that Handel should have written *tasto solo* if he intended the bare octaves. (In *Glory to God,* for instance, the tenor and bass passage—' And peace on earth '—is marked *tasto solo.*) On the other hand the original bass line is clear of figuring. Imaginatively, the indeterminate and groping effect of the music, to which Burney referred, is enhanced with transitory modulations implied rather than stated.

For unto us: con rip. bars 1 to first beat of 7th bar, 33—37, 49—53, 68—end.

Pastoral Symphony or *Pifa:* this is richly disposed; violin I with violin III an octave lower; violin II and viola an octave lower; *senza rip.* throughout. The most illuminating detail is the division *à* 3 of the violins. Wind additions to this movement are an insolence. Handel did not want the actual but the ideal. Not Italian bagpipes but the illusion of heavenly bagpipes. ' Mozart introduced piccolo, flute, oboes, clarinets, bassoons and horns to suggest the sound of bagpipes.' That was an error of judgement.

There were shepherds—And suddenly: strings (*senza rip.*) bowed thus in *And lo:* violins

violas

and also cellos, which are mostly in unison with the violas.

And suddenly is unbowed. It should be, therefore, *staccato* or *semi-staccato*. Thus the music *shines*.

Glory to God: with *ripieno* instruments, but with trumpets carefully kept *da lontano*.

Rejoice: violin and cello *senza rip*.

He shall feed His flock: string ensemble. This is not marked, but one would assume *senza rip*.

His yoke is easy: there is exquisite interplay between the two groups. *Senza rip*. 1—10 (second beat), 11 (last beat)—14 (second beat), 15 (last three quavers) —18 (seventh quaver), 20—22 (seventh quaver), 25 —29 (third quaver). The *ripieno* enter with

(34—35) and are answered by the solo instruments

From 36—the end *tutti*.

Behold the Lamb of God: con rip. from bar 4 (2nd beat).

He was despised: 2 violins, viola, cello *senza rip.*

Surely: con rip. from bar 6.

And with His stripes: con rip. from bar 19—bass entry.

All we like sheep: con rip. from bar 2.

All they that see Him: violins, viola, cello *senza rip.* Note: Handel marks the top line ' violin 1 and 2 ', the second line ' violin 3 '.

He trusted in God: con rip.

Thy rebuke: a *recitativo secco* is set in a frame of string tone. *Senza rip.*

Behold and see: senza rip. Notice the effect of the viola in the opening bars.

He was cut off: as *Thy rebuke.*

But Thou didst not leave: a serene duet between solo violin and voice. Keep the bass very smooth.

Lift up your heads: The antiphony between high and low voices is matched by *concertino* with the one and *tutti* with the other. From bar 30 to end *tutti.*

Let all the angels: all strings throughout.

Thou art gone up on high: duet between voice and violin with cello and continuo.

The Lord gave the word: con rip, per tutto.

How beautiful are the feet: duet between voice and violin I, with cello and continuo.

Their sound is gone out: con rip. from bar 4.

Why do the nations: Strings *senza rip.* The effect of the rhythmic precision possible with a small group *plus* continuo is electrifying. The vocal coloratura is not obscured. Mozart added flutes, oboes, bassoons, trumpets and drums.

Let us break their bonds: con rip. from bar 3.

Thou shalt break them: again the absolute clarity of
solo violin *plus* cello and continuo is extraordinarily
telling.

Hallelujah: the *ripieno* instruments enter in the middle
of the fifth bar. Thus one learns to aim at brightness
at the outset, reserving weight for the entry of trumpets and drums.

I know that my Redeemer liveth: Translucently scored
for solo violin, cello and continuo. A recent critic
observed that one violin was not sufficiently impersonal. The whole, Protestant, point surely is that the
expression is essentially personal—'I know that *my*
Redeemer liveth'. I'm sorry but later additions to
the scoring merely make for sentimentality. The
origin of the music is Italian. Preserve the Italian
character and refrain from adding too much of the
German.

By man came also and *Even so in Christ: con rip.*

Behold, I tell you a mystery and *The trumpet shall
sound:* strings *con rip.* Note the vivid rhythmic
flashes in the strings. The solo trumpeter should
remember that he is accompanying a singer and
should treat the high notes with as much discretion
as possible.

O death where is thy sting: continuo and cello only.

The remaining choruses are *con rip,* throughout, and
If God be for us follows the familiar pattern of
violin with cello, continuo and voice.

Reversion to Handelian scoring means dullness only

if the letter is observed at the expense of the spirit. The devotees of Mr Britten (among whom I must be numbered) will recognise that forceful musical expression comes with more compulsion from few rather than from many instruments. The small, disciplined force controls enormous resources of power. More than this, it has certain reserves of expression denied to a large body. We must approach our Handel score as we approach Britten—or for that matter Bach, whose respectability generally deters the vandals from rewriting his major works.

It is certain that the music of the mid-eighteenth century has lightness, delicacy, and brilliance not to be surpassed by any other music. Handel's orchestra is not an inferior precursor of the ' modern ' orchestra: it is the culmination of the Italian renaissance ensemble. It stands, therefore as a peak. The eminence of this orchestration is to be appreciated with relief— and with respect.

There are practical problems to consider. There is no standard set of parts in circulation. It is possible to compare the existing parts with Chrysander's full score, made for the German Handel Society in 1901, and to edit them accordingly. If subtractions are made from Prout's edition of 1902 in accordance with the notes given above a reasonable degree of accuracy will be achieved. Absolute authenticity, for reasons already stated, is not to be achieved, but the right balance and proportions may.

CONCLUSION

IT WOULD BE stupid to suppose that wholesale conversion to the standards suggested is likely. So long as our vast choral societies function the annual *Messiah* will furnish funds for the adventurous to present other works to half empty houses at other periods of the year than Christmas. Such societies should, however, regard *Messiah* as a work of difficulty, both technical and intellectual. Each performance should be contemplated as a new experience. The conductor should try to see Handel behind Mozart, Hiller, Franz, Smithers or Prout and emphasise, despite the alien orchestral character, the particular qualities of Handel. Above all he should see the work as a unity.

Messiah might well be a work from which applause is eliminated. At least as a temporary measure this would be salutary for the performers who like to indulge their vanity at the expense of musical integrity.

For the small town society (where intelligent appreciation is often higher than in the large town in which visiting virtuosi have wrecked legitimate self-esteem) the slighter forces Handel had are a recommendation. (1) There is much less expense. (2) A good deal of out-of-tune playing is eliminated. (3) String players, who form the basis of any local orchestra, play much better when divorced from wind which often distracts attention from string inefficiency by its more noticeable defects.

Engage a good professional string quartet, who will play the *senza rip.* portions. Let the *ripieno* players concentrate on what is left. There is quite enough.

If possible—this for chapels and churches—reduce expenditure on ' big names ' and concentrate on the accompaniment. Too often the engagement of a ' big name ' fails to stipulate the artistry that should be there. Some expensive performances are disgraceful. There are, of course, many honourable exceptions.

Avoid, if possible, accompaniment of the whole oratorio by organ alone. It is very wearisome. The accompaniment as laid out by Best or Prout is, additionally, very difficult. Organ (or piano) and no more than string quartet—if nothing more is available—is quite enough to reveal the outlines of the work.

I was delighted, the other day, when a country cottage in my home village was reprieved. Motor cars will be forced to go slower. But the sixteenth century will continue to smile. Another age stands with another point of view. So with Handel. His point of view is different from ours. We can teach him nothing. He can teach us much. He needs no intermediaries.